Ten Poems
of Hope

Candlestick Press

Published by:

Candlestick Press,
Diversity House, 72 Nottingham Road, Arnold, Nottingham NG5 6LF
www.candlestickpress.co.uk

Design and typesetting by Craig Twigg

Printed by Ratcliff & Roper Print Group, Nottinghamshire, UK

Selection © Di Slaney and Kathy Towers, 2022

Cover illustration © Sarah Kirby, 2022
www.sarahkirby.co.uk

Candlestick Press monogram © Barbara Shaw, 2008

© Candlestick Press, 2022

ISBN 978 1 913627 20 1

Acknowledgements

The poems in this pamphlet are reprinted from the following books, all by permission of the publishers listed unless stated otherwise. Every effort has been made to trace the copyright holders of the poems published in this book. The editor and publisher apologise if any material has been included without permission or without the appropriate acknowledgement, and would be glad to be told of anyone who has not been consulted.

Thanks are due to all the copyright holders cited below for their kind permission:

Fleur Adcock, *Poems 1960-2000* (Bloodaxe Books, 2000) www.bloodaxebooks.com. Sujata Bhatt, *Monkey Shadows* (Carcanet Press Ltd, 1991). Kerry Hardie, *Selected Poems* (Gallery Press, 2011) by kind permission of the author and The Gallery Press, Loughcrew, Oldcastle, County Meath, Ireland. Roy Marshall, *The Sun Bathers* (Shoestring Press, 2013) by kind permission of the author and Shoestring Press. Paula Meehan, *As If By Magic: Selected Poems* (Dedalus Press, 2020). Roger Robinson, *A Portable Paradise* (Peepal Tree Press, 2019). Laura Theis, poem first published in the Winchester Poetry Prize 2022, by kind permission of the author. Katie Dunstan, poem first published in this pamphlet, by kind permission of the author.

All permissions cleared courtesy of Dr Suzanne Fairless-Aitken
c/o Swift Permissions swiftpermissions@gmail.com

Where poets are no longer living, their dates are given.

A Portable Paradise

And if I speak of Paradise,
then I'm speaking of my grandmother
who told me to carry it always
on my person, concealed, so
no one else would know but me.
That way they can't steal it, she'd say.
And if life puts you under pressure,
trace its ridges in your pocket,
smell its piney scent on your handkerchief,
hum its anthem under your breath.
And if your stresses are sustained and daily,
get yourself to an empty room – be it hotel,
hostel or hovel – find a lamp
and empty your paradise onto a desk:
your white sands, green hills and fresh fish.
Shine the lamp on it like the fresh hope
of morning, and keep staring at it till you sleep.

Roger Robinson

Boats in the Bay

I will take my trouble and wrap it in a blue handkerchief
And carry it down to the sea.
The sea is as smooth as silk, is as silent as glass;
It does not even whisper
Only the boats, rowed out by the girls in yellow
Ruffle its surface.
It is grey, not blue. It is flecked with boats like midges,
With happy people
Moving soundlessly over the level water.

I will take my trouble and drop it into the water
It is heavy as stone and smooth as a sea-washed pebble.
It will sink under the sea, and the happy people
Will row over it quietly, ruffling the clear water
Little dark boats like midges, skimming silently
Will pass backwards and forwards, the girls singing;
They will never know that they have sailed above sorrow.
Sink heavily and lie still, lie still my trouble.

Winifred Holtby (1898 – 1935)

Instant Karma

The office cleaner sings beautifully and in Hindi.
I ask her what her song means.

"The Lord says, I will give you what you want
when the time is right."

She leaves a world bright with belief,
the mopped floor under my feet,

the emptied bin of me.

Roy Marshall

Say not the Struggle Nought Availeth

Say not the struggle nought availeth,
    The labour and the wounds are vain,
The enemy faints not, nor faileth,
    And as things have been, things remain.

If hopes were dupes, fears may be liars;
    It may be, in yon smoke concealed,
Your comrades chase e'en now the fliers,
    And, but for you, possess the field.

For while the tired waves, vainly breaking,
    Seem here no painful inch to gain,
Far back through creeks and inlets making
    Comes, silent, flooding in, the main,

And not by eastern windows only,
    When daylight comes, comes in the light,
In front the sun climbs slow, how slowly,
    But westward, look, the land is bright.

Arthur Hugh Clough (1819 – 1861)

Song of the Open Road

I

Afoot and light-hearted I take to the open road,
Healthy, free, the world before me,
The long brown path before me leading wherever I choose.

Henceforth I ask not good-fortune, I myself am good-fortune,
Henceforth I whimper no more, postpone no more, need nothing,
Done with indoor complaints, libraries, querulous criticisms,
Strong and content I travel the open road.

The earth, that is sufficient,
I do not want the constellations any nearer,
I know they are very well where they are,
I know they suffice for those who belong to them,

(Still here I carry my old delicious burdens,
I carry them, men and women, I carry them with me wherever I go,
I swear it is impossible for me to get rid of them,
I am fill'd with them, and I will fill them in return.)

Walt Whitman (1819 – 1892)

For Andrew

'Will I die?' you ask. And so I enter on
The dutiful exposition of that which you
Would rather not know, and I rather not tell you.
To soften my 'Yes' I offer compensations –
Age and fulfilment ('It's so far away;
You will have children and grandchildren by then')
And indifference ('By then you will not care').
No need: you cannot believe me, convinced
That if you always eat plenty of vegetables
And are careful crossing the street you will live for ever.
And so we close the subject, with much unsaid –
This, for instance: Though you and I may die
Tomorrow or next year, and nothing remain
Of our stock, of the unique, preciously-hoarded
Inimitable genes we carry in us,
It is possible that for many generations
There will exist, sprung from whatever seeds,
Children straight-limbed, with clear enquiring voices,
Bright-eyed as you. Or so I like to think:
Sharing in this your childish optimism.

Fleur Adcock

29 April 1989

She's three-months-old now,
asleep at last for the afternoon.
I've got some time to myself again
but I don't know what to do.
Outside everything is greyish green and soggy
with endless Bremen-Spring drizzle.
I make a large pot of Assam tea
and search through the books
in my room, shift through my papers.
I'm not looking for anything, really,
just touching favourite books.
I don't even know what I'm thinking,
but there's a rich round fullness
in the air
like living inside Beethoven's piano
on a day when he was
particularly energetic.

Sujata Bhatt

My Father Perceived as a Vision of St Francis
for Brendan Kennelly

It was the piebald horse in next door's garden
frightened me out of a dream
with her dawn whinny. I was back
in the boxroom of the house,
my brother's room now,
full of ties and sweaters and secrets.
Bottles chinked on the doorstep,
the first bus pulled up to the stop.
The rest of the house slept

except for my father. I heard
him rake the ash from the grate,
plug in the kettle, hum a snatch of a tune.
Then he unlocked the back door
and stepped out into the garden.

Autumn was nearly done, the first frost
whitened the slates of the estate.
He was older than I had reckoned,
his hair completely silver,
and for the first time I saw the stoop
of his shoulder, saw that
his leg was stiff. What's he at?
So early and still stars in the west?

They came then: birds
of every size, shape, colour; they came
from the hedges and shrubs,
from eaves and garden sheds,
from the industrial estate, outlying fields,
from Dubber Cross they came
and the ditches of the North Road.

The garden was a pandemonium
when my father threw up his hands
and tossed the crumbs in the air. The sun

cleared O'Reilly's chimney
and he was suddenly radiant,
a perfect vision of St Francis,
made whole, made young again,
in a Finglas garden.

Paula Meehan

Some things I like
after Lemn Sissay

I like tall trees, I like crunchy orange leaves,
I like lying back in calm seas,
I like hugs, I like pastel mugs,
I like the way the bottle glugs,
I like acknowledgements in books;
For my Grandmothers. For Jane. For my Dad,
who taught me about hope.

I like brush strokes, I like crap jokes,
I like people who applaud runny yolks,
I like colourful wool, I like the way joy is full,
I like pockets and finding lockets
with photographs cut perfectly to size,
I like four am skies,
he likes my eyes
when I talk about anything
I love,
I like how above clouds the sky
is always blue,
I like a bench with a view
and the *dedicated to* that stops us
week
on
week,

To Serayen,
free and fearless on his eternal
bear hunt.

I like people who sing out loud,
I like how birds never crowd,
they flock,
I like an unmatched sock,
I like red lips, I like vinegar soaked chips,
I like the way the sun
drips,

I like just sitting awhile,
I like a stranger's smile,
I like swings, I like statement rings,
I like how great friends give you wings.

I like imagining crows in slippers,
cats wearing flippers,
I like how ducks believe puddles are oceans, wow,
how incredible is that?

Katie Dunstan

I went out today looking for wonder

Found a wind,
two ducks.

Fifteen clouds shaped like
questions containing their own answer,

the way only water
can shapeshift itself.

I found a tree that had decided to start its spring early,
regardless of the general consensus.

I found a stick that had made
a dog's morning.

I found a well-rested sun with a six-hour workday
and a penchant for early nights.

Cycling back home on the towpath at nightfall,
I startled water rats.

The moon was a luminous finger nail
reflected below in the darkness to both sides of my wheels.

The flooding had turned the river
into a mirror, the meadows into a lake.

I wanted to show it to you,
each incredible marvel, and say:

Look, oh, look,
see how the good world still holds you.

Laura Theis

Afterword

May
for Marian

The blessèd stretch and ease of it –
heart's ease. The hills blue. All the flowering weeds
bursting open. Balm in the air.
The birdsong bouncing back out of the sky. The cattle
lain down in the meadow, forgetting to feed.
The horses swishing their tails.
The yellow flare of furze on the near hill.
And the first cream splatters of blossom
high on the thorns where the day rests longest.

All hardship, hunger, treachery of winter
forgotten.
This unfounded conviction: forgiveness, hope.

Kerry Hardie